NAKED

Jessica Suthers

Presentation by *BookLeaf Publishing*

Web: www.bookleafpub.com

E-mail: info@bookleafpub.com

ISBN: 9789395950367

First edition 2023

RAIN DROPS

Rain drops on the tin roof, it feels like home
Rain drops on my skin, I don't care if I'm alone
Rain drops clear away all the pain
Rain drops one by one make me feel sane

LOVE

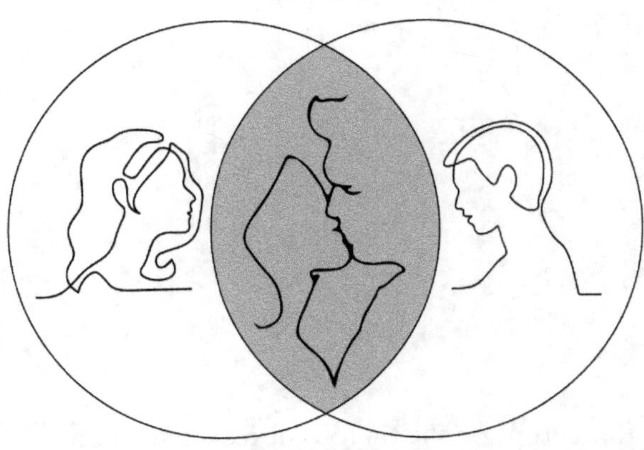

Loving you was something I didn't want to do
No matter how much I ran from it,
I kept coming back to you
Loving you won't be easy, I know.
But loving you is better than the winter snow
It warms me up, it takes my breath
You make me realize, I deserve nothing less.
Loving you feels so natural
I'm just hoping that it doesn't
come with any.. collateral- damage
Don't leave me empty, like a famine.
Don't make me have to re-examine,
The way I love you.

CANDLE WITHIN

Flickering
but holding strong
internal battles sing like a song,
flickering.
my candle still burning.
my soul's on fire… yearning.
yearning to be set free
let me roam the world, just to be me
let me go.. let me go.. let me go ..
there's no place like home
and my homes within.
let me walk the land that my past lives
have been
flickering
but I refuse to go out
setting myself free erasing all the doubt.

burn baby…grow baby
no ifs.. ands.. buts or maybes
let it shine, apologetically
Walk that walk and talk that talk even when it's
heavy
that light is heavenly
believe it or not it comes with ease
This is your destiny,
so believe in me
no longer flickering yet lit up with ease
hold that flame
let it transmute your pain
let that fire
cleanse you
warm you
comfort you
and guide you
it's the gift from the most high that you pray to
"this little light of mine I'm gonna let it shine"
so let it shine
in a world of darkness it's here to lead the blind
So ease your mind you're not losing it
they might call you crazy but they've never been
through it
as long as you INNERstand it doesn't matter
who UNDERstands
it's either beneath OR above you
so put it in JAHS hands
your flame is burning

your soul is yearning
go out and fulfill your book
don't be ashamed to be overlooked
let that light shine
it's all going to happen in Divine timing, from a
flicker to ablaze.
admire it in a-maze-meant

This light is heaven sent.

HERE'S TO YOU

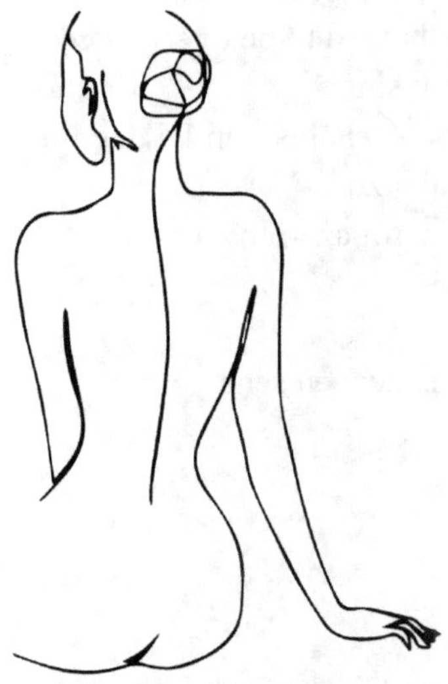

The brighter the light the darker shadow
you come to me for insight but refuse to see my
sorrow
I'm trying to change—embrace love but that's a
bit hard when I'm afraid of what I made of
it's too hard to be happy all the time I've come
to accept that it's okay to cry
admit that I'm a little touched deprived
I've had thoughts of suicide
I wanted to die…but not really die
just kill off this version that I feel inside
the one that lies
the one who is not good at goodbyes
the one who got attachment issues

the one who pushes people away… then
immediately misses you
the one who dealt with everything we've ever
been through
choose fight or flight… she flew
The truth is I need to bless you,
hold you,
kiss and caress you.
admire and respect you
Because you get us through
through all the things meant to:
Deplete us
Drain us
Stop us
Destroy us
because of you I find it hard to trust
I think everyone's against us
you are my protection
but we're trying for Ascension
with that I'll let you to rest
take a break from all of the test
take a look at all of our progress
realize that we are truly blessed
take a rest.
take a breath, make the plan
set a date
teach me how to incorporate..
you
let me show you how much we grew

believe in ourselves the only way to the truth
it's a bumpy road they can't all be smooth
get back up…get back in your groove
focus on what you want, that's your truth
listen for God's word, and then make a move.
rest in silence and Solitude
Here's to you.
Here's to you.

GREEN 7

The way the golden hour illuminates your face
you're like my perfect mistake
Eyes, golden pools of honey
make me dream of the lifetime where you used
to hold me
the first time I saw you
I knew this wasn't something out of the blue
I know that I've known you
in every life
I know that I've always been your wife
but this time..this time it was different we were
separated to try and make it all make sense
this lifetime was for both of us to heal
 process all these emotions learn how to really
feel
I always feel you in my heart

I know you're there even in the middle of the
dark
Your mere existence, your path crossing mine
gave me a reason to look forward to my next
lifetime
to love..to cherish..to adorn you
I accept everything that is of you
you are fire you are earth..water…and wind
with each other we are destined to Win
but in this life I will love you from a distance
you're my motivation to keep consistent
I just say that you do the same
so one day soon the separation won't be in vain
I know with you as my partner
there's no moment in space that we won't
Charter
my love..my light…my king…
I would allow you to be my everything
Adam and Eve, made from your rib
I will bless you with a home full of kids
fulfilling your deepest legacies
giving you all of my love, fulfilling our
prophecies
love you deeply…passionately…unconditionally
I was made for you, and you for me
spend hours using you as my muse
1 million words couldn't describe the way that I
love you

I think about you, skin to skin dreaming of you
your last name as to be one of your kin
in this life we were born full of sin maybe in the
next we will be born again
then I will have you again
but until then…
it's until we meet again
-amor

BALANCE

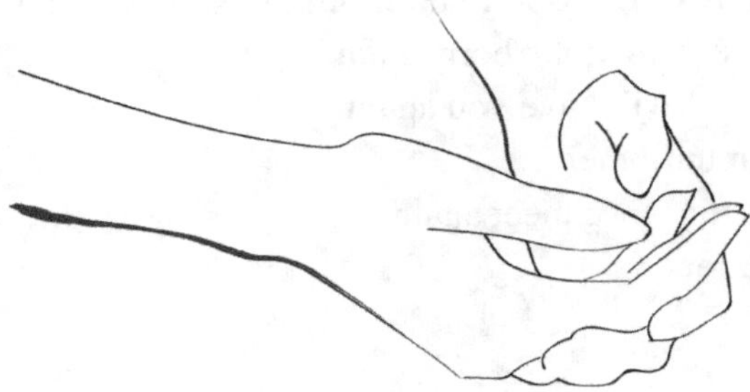

Balance
two syllables, seven letter
embody that life would be better
every step taken the scales seem to tip
I begin the question if I'm even well equipped
to handle this mission…this destiny Begin to
question why did he breathe this on to me
How did I become worthy —-
when I can't even balance
I'm feeling stagnant
what's the plan big G? I gotta have it
I'm losing my balance
I can fill it take over but I don't want to give into
the habit..
Dear God, send me my balance.

N. A. K. E. D

NAKED
Never
Acting but
Knowingly
Embodying
Divinity
NAKED
mask off
this is me and my power
 where were you in my Darkest Hour
love me…NAKED
or don't love me at all
you were gone as soon as you saw me begin to
fall
NAKED
under all the skin and bones

deep down where my soul glows
where my light is blinding
my love forever binding
NAKED
can you love me on the darkest days
where my smile doesn't show and my light
begins to fade
NAKED
down to my core
can you accept me, all of me that pours?
behind all of this standing
NAKED
this is the key to my true bliss
 NAKED
explore my mind
NAKED
my body
NAKED
my soul
NAKED
Never
Acting but
Knowingly
Embodying
Divinity

NAKED

JUST THE THREE OF US

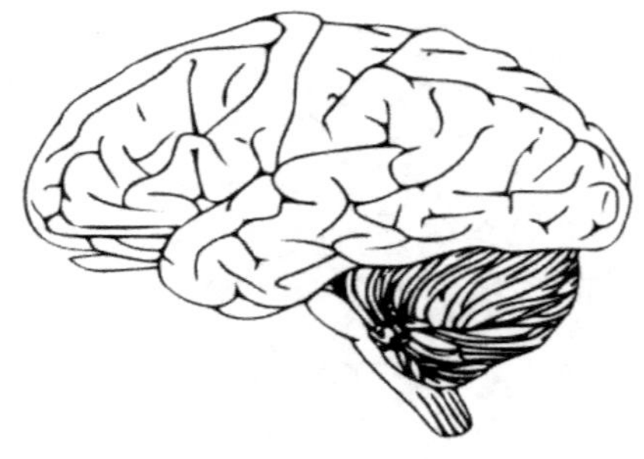

Me myself and I
Encompassing all three, it's a hell of a ride
When one falls the other 2 rise
Just me myself and I
It's all we've ever had
Through the good ugly and the bad
We don't know how to let anyone in
The only time we feel safe is within
Me myself and I
Even on the days when one wanted to die
It was just me myself and I
Just the three of us
Protecting the mind body and soul
Learning how to trust
Letting go of the old
Just me myself and I until the very end
I've got you and you got me friend
Just me myself and I

MISDIAGNOSED

diagnosed bipolar
but it was really an inner child that was
desperate to hold her
a little touch deprived
nervous system all fucked up
because I was just trying to survive
I had to regulate myself
take all of those feelings that weren't mine,
and put them on a shelf
I had to isolate
Learn to be myself and create, bake, and eat my
own cake
stop trying to please the world

and take care of the one inside because I love
that baby girl
I had to take off my cape
I wore the title of captain save a h** like it was
my last day
but I got tired
all I do now is stay in my lane and squire
write it all down
because when I feel like I'm about to drown
getting it on pen and paper makes me feel found
I read it enough to realize how profound,
that I sound.
Misdiagnosed, anxiety
When I was really surrounding—myself with
people who wanted to see the light inside of me,
die.
I spent my whole life just trying to survive
thinking there was something wrong with me
but it was really what was around me
that was stopping me from my destiny
trying to put a label on me
so that I would be conceived is crazy
like my brain didn't work properly
like I was supposed to be ashamed of what was
me
like I needed to change what was me
but I just had to take a step back and then I could
breathe
and then my thoughts calm down

my heart slows down

I notice myself day by day I'm no longer
drown-ing
I just had to start believing in me
and is my job to fulfill my prophecy
and it's my job to leave the legacy
and it's my job to never lose me - again

LOSING YOU

I won't allow myself to love you when the only thing you're capable of is breaking my heart. Everything sinks the second we're apart. And the butterflies fade the smile disappears as the tears reappear. I can't do this can't live in fear, the only thing I'm afraid of is losing you my dear.

HURT

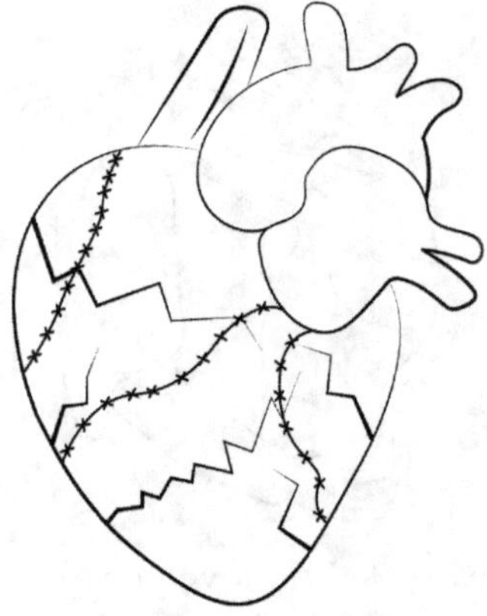

You said it wouldn't hurt. But to me it feels as if someone has cracked open my chest, stole my heart, and continue to play and twist it until it's so tattered and torn that it's about to break in two. Is this not hurt I feel?

I'M SORRY

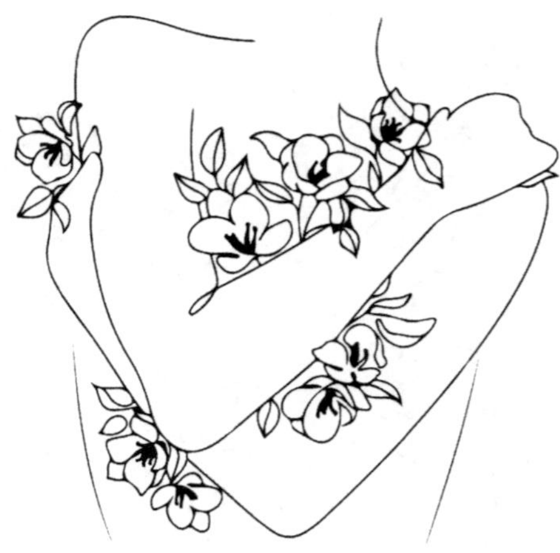

Then vs now I'm sorry Baby Girl, for not loving you the way I should have then, but I no longer run in shame I embrace you for who you were. I love you for who you felt you had to be. You're resilient, courageous, and a force to be reckoned with. I'm happy that I've learned to love you and cherish you the way you should have been all along. I see the beauty in every inch I use to critique. You can rest now. I got it from here.

SEX BETTER THAN LOVE

People say, "sex ain't better than love" but, why
not believe in something that's real, rather than
something that's made up?
What does it even mean to love
Is it something that I even need to be afraid of
Is it something that truly fills you up inside
Something that makes you swallow all your
demons, especially your pride
See this is all new to me
The only thing I've ever known is how someone
can use me
Abuse me
"Love" me then leave me
Use me for everything that is my body

Never wanting to understand my mind
Just be conquered and able to "call you mine"
But I've heard of a love that's different, a love
that is divine
It comes with patience, it comes with time
But when you get it, dear God it is so fine
Like an aged wine
Stout, yet sweet
Like the wind beneath your Wings
Being swept from your feet
All your inner demons, they get defeat-ed-
silenced
You don't have to ask plead or beg
It all comes together
You're able to storm any weather
Able to get through all the good bad and better
Floating in happiness Light as a feather
So maybe sex isn't better
Just something to add to the top
Not a reason to stop
but a way to get deeper
Deeper into each other, knowing their ins and
outs
Understanding their mind and all their doubts
Truly loving them
From start to finish, bringing to end
Falling in love with your best friend.

PAPER CHASE

Everyone is on a paper chase that never stops. They always want more and more, filling themselves with greed. Forgetting where they came from, the morals they were raised with, and any form of empathy.

INSOMNIA

Hello insomnia, my old friend
Tonight we meet again
I can't say that I've missed you
In all reality I can't stand you
You make my Brain wither away
Confuse my nights with my days
Oh god dear insomnia
You're quite a bitch
You leave me feeling as if I have an itch
And itch I can't scratch
Nothing helps
No medicine bottle on the shelf
Makes you go away
So I accept however long you choose to stay
Maybe it's for a reason

Maybe you're coming to visit just for a season
I just hate how you make my mind wander
I would much rather be in a deep slumber
Oh you dear friend
Why do we have to meet again

LA LUNA

It's the way you illuminate every shadow, command attention when you arrive, heal the hearts of those who are open, and make me thankful I'm alive.

Your beauty has held my attention, ever since I opened my eyes. The love you omit is a pure conviction, and I pray it never dies.

Your mothering spirit holds me at night, and pushed me through my darkest times.

You remind me to never dim my light, and to wipe the tears from my eyes.

I hold you dear with honor and glory and release
all of the worry
With every changing phase we go through,
I say my goodbyes with the morning dew.

Until we meet again my dear friend

-

DEMONS

I'm fighting demons everyday, and even if you wanted to, I wouldn't want you to stay. Can you see? See the things you've done to me? But now I'm gone I've found a way to be free. I just want to be left alone, you're the reason I have all these voices in my dome. Not much more that I can take. The pain inside your chest that's what it feels like for your heart to break. Trust me I would know that. Because you shattered mine a long time ago for a matter of fact. But you, you still try. Try everything inside you to bring me down. But you can't because I once was lost but now I'm found.

THE PATH

Some roads you have to take alone
No hand in yours, no crowd, not even stoned
Just you and god that's all
It gets hard and you'll even fall
But you get back up and you keep fighting
Because there is something in you that needs
some dying
Purge it out
Kick scream and shout
Just get it out

I WOKE UP WITH YOU ON MY MIND AGAIN..

Woke up with you on my mind again
Very grateful and thankful to call you a friend
Your smile your laugh and even your grin
It's intoxicatin

On this beautiful day I pray for you
May you be filled with light and never blue
Even on the bad days know he walks with you
And everything you've been through-
Was to get you through
To this very point in time
Use all the dark to let your light shine- bright
Do it all, despite- any pain
Because even the most beautiful flowers still
need the rain.

be blessed love
And please never give up.

I'm rooting for you
Cloaked in protection like the morning grass
with dew
List all your gratitudes

Make today the best you can, it's all in your attitude.
When you make your list start with the most important… you ♥

RIVER ROCK

beautifully smooth and found in the depths of
the water
the only way that I got this way was to go with
the flow
let the water overtake me
smooth all my rough edges and sand me

down with Grace flow
not caring which direction we were to go
just to flow
flow in the river Let the water take over
bumping my edges along the way across every
bank chipping away
a little bit at a time and
at first it seem sad like you're losing a piece of
you
but the thing is all it's doing is breaking the
guard down that surrounds you
the guard that didn't need to be there in the
protection that wasn't needed just going with the
flow of the water in every season
 hot and cold all of it is what formed me and
allowed me
 to be on display so beautifully

the soft smooth edges I would like to talk and
tell the story
of everything
everything I went through after all the things
that truly didn't matter but it chipped off for me
Formed me into this River rock

THE LAST TIME

If I knew that the last time was gonna be the last
time I would've done things different
Held you a little closer kissed you a little longer
made it a little more innocent.
if I knew the last time was going to be the last
time
I would've spent that time creating a lifetime
-with you
but I didn't know that the last time was going to
be the last time so I'm sitting here missing you
thinking of you re-creating every moment and
every breath that I took with you it's the simple
things
I wanted to love you so bad but there were so
many strings
I wanted to love you so bad but I couldn't
confess to you

so I just sit here and let it sting
but I really just want to let it out I want to sing
sing Sweet melodies sit and think about all the
Ifs and maybes
sit and think about if you were my baby
if I knew that the last time was gonna be the last
time I would've found a way to stop time
find a way to wrap your arms around mine
find a way to capture the divine
if I knew the last time was going to be the last
time I would pause the frame
and not let it all go in vain
Hold you tight and whisper your name but I
guess it's all the same
because even though the last time was the last
time the only person who knew how I felt was
the one in my mind
for whatever reason I felt like loving you was a
crime
but it's one that I was willing to do the time -for
Say I'll let you walk in and out like my heart is
this revolving door
and then love you in silence and I'm stuck
crying -on the floor
scream eternally until my throat sore because for
whatever reason I can't come up with the
courage to tell you how I truly feel
I have this thought that you're going to make it a
big deal

and I would rather love you in silence hurt in
private
then to take the chance of opening up and have
you say goodbye-but ..
who really wins in the end
because I'm sitting here thinking that I love you
but I don't want you to stop being my friend
watch the sun come up lay in the same spot from
dusk till dawn
being careful with my moves and protect the
queen at all costs; let go of the pawns.
Check mate

www.ingramcontent.com/pod-product-compliance
Lightning Source LLC
LaVergne TN
LVHW010929200726
843509LV00013B/2141